How to Survive
When One Twin Dies

One woman's journey through
twin loss during pregnancy

Vicky Burley

Published by The Loving Parent

ISBN 978-1-482-76540-3

Dedicated to Coran Engyl Smith whose little life touched those of so many others. We are blessed that you entered our lives and eternally grateful that you were in them, even for such a short period of time.

Table of Contents

Introduction

On 12th May 2005, we discovered that we were expecting twins. Moments later, we were told that one of them was unlikely to survive the pregnancy.

I wrote a journal during the months that followed, as a means to express the many conflicting emotions I was experiencing and a way of keeping my friends and family informed of our progress.

The pages that follow are those journal entries.

I have a strong memory of feeling lonely during the period. Although I eventually found support online, there were no books, manuals or information to help me through the difficult time. I hope that by sharing my story in this way, other parents who are faced with similar situations find some strength and solace in discovering that they are not alone. I hope that they will discover that it is not only possible to survive the grief, but to ultimately thrive despite it.

Wishing you love. And peace.

Vicky
March 2013

1st June – The First Few Days

It was Thursday 12th May when we found out that we were expecting twins but that there was a complication.

On 9th January, we had been delighted to discover I was pregnant. We'd been 'trying' for no more than three weeks and felt ever so proud that we'd been so very efficient! I knew that 2005 was the year that I wanted to have a baby. I'd been suggesting it to Jeremy for a while and on Winter Solstice, he turned to me and said, "Let's make a baby!" Little did we know that the magic of that day actually created two.

Twenty-two weeks later I was lying on a couch in a darkened room at East Surrey Hospital with gooey jelly smeared on my rotund belly.

We had decided not to have a scan at 10 weeks: We were confident of our 'dates' (I have always kept a record of when I menstruate) and felt that the outcome of a Nuchal Translucency Scan (the test for ascertaining the probability of Down's Syndrome) would not affect our choices for the pregnancy. There was, of course, the temptation to see our baby 'for real' for the first time but in the end decided that this was a selfish motivation and not one that benefited the babe in any way.

That was a great decision. Had we had the scan, we would have found out that there were twins, but not that there was a problem. Three months of preparing for twins would have followed before the 'developmental' scan at around 20 weeks.

Very early on in the pregnancy, Jeremy had noticed in one of my numerous pregnancy books that in the early weeks, an embryo looks rather like a peanut! So the name stuck. 'Peanut' became a part of our lives. I was sure that Peanut was a boy; a steely, determined, probably stubborn and yet wise little boy. Jeremy thought that Peanut was a girl. Either way, we didn't mind. And we didn't want to know until the moment of birth.

My sisters and I had all been born at home. At three years old, I had the privilege of attending my sister's very first birthday! As she crowned, I stroked her head and said, "Hello, little one! Are you a boy or a girl?" I remember it well. I don't remember any screaming or pain or blood. I only recall the magic of my little baby sister being born into our world.

Unfortunately I missed my other sister's birth by a matter of minutes. I was a big girl of five by then and remember peeking through the gap at the side of the door trying to see what was going on. Of course, my mother saw me straightaway and invited me into the room. I remember lots of grown-ups around my parents' bed and my beautiful mummy lying on the bed with my new baby sister in her arms. She had a full head of hair and looked so calm and peaceful. I was a proud big sister once again.

I'd always known that I'd wanted a home birth with as little intervention as possible. I'd seen homeopathic remedies 'in action' when I attended the labour and delivery of one of my patients in February 2004. She'd had an emergency C-section with her last baby, who was an undiagnosed breech and so was thrilled to be able to have a vaginal delivery with no intervention or pain killers, except for a little gas and air (she said it made her feel funny) and the homeopathic remedies that I prescribed. Once again, my experience – as an observer – of labour and delivery was one of joy, love and the nature of woman working at its best.

At my booking-in appointment, I was thrilled to find out that Julie, my midwife, had been born at home herself and was very supportive of home births in low-risk pregnancies such as mine. The appointment lasted an hour and a half whilst a lovely student midwife, Jackie, took copious details from Jeremy and I – about our health, our families, our domestic situation, our work and of course our hopes for the pregnancy and delivery.

One of the questions we were asked was whether or not there were twins in our family. I recounted that my paternal grandmother Blanche was an identical twin to Mary and that my second cousins, John and Edward were identical twins. I stated how lovely I thought it would be to have twins and Jackie joked as she wrote, "Hoping for twins!"

From very early on I had a feeling that I was pregnant with twins. When I read the pregnancy books, it seemed that my pregnancy symptoms were all coming a week or two earlier than the 'norm'. By the time I was nine weeks pregnant, I could no longer wear my normal trousers and my breasts had swelled to unrecognisable proportions! When the midwife examined the height of the fundus, I was always two or three weeks bigger than the 'norm' for my gestation time. These things backed up the feeling that perhaps we had two Peanuts, after all. But when I imagined our future, when I envisaged how our family would be, I only ever saw Jeremy and I with one baby. So I put any thought of twins to the back of mind. I joked about it with Jeremy every now and again, but I never really took it seriously.

Within a minute of lying on the ultrasonographer's couch, we were told that we had twins. I turned to Jeremy and shrieked! A million thoughts went through my head in that moment. Would it be double trouble or double the joy? We'd have to buy another cot, a different buggy. Could we afford the nursery costs for two babies? Can you breastfeed two babies? How would we cope? But the flow of thoughts was stopped very quickly when the ultrasonographer told us that she thought she could see a potential problem. At first sight, it looked like 'Twin 2' was very much smaller than 'Twin 1'.

For the next 15 minutes or so, we saw pictures of 'Twin 1' on the monitor. What an extraordinary experience. It is a wonderful thing to be able to see a picture of your unborn child. The measurements were taken, the heart examined, the skin and organs all found to be intact and developing properly. All seemed to be in order.

Our attentions were then turned to 'Twin 2'. It was immediately apparent how much smaller this little baby was. The ultrasonographer spent no more than five minutes looking for internal structures but very quickly decided that it would be better for us to be referred to a specialist centre for a second opinion. We did, however, see that the heart was beating strong. I will never forget that image.

The ultrasonagrapher told us very little about the problem – only that it looked like the baby's brain hadn't developed properly and that she thought it unlikely that it would survive. She then left the room to book an appointment with St George's Hospital in Tooting.

I said 'Sorry' to Jeremy and burst into tears. Of course, he told me never to apologise again and that it wasn't my fault, before wrapping his strong arms around me and holding me firm whilst our tears flooded each other's faces. For a few glorious moments we had rejoiced in the knowledge that we had twins only to be faced with any parent's worst nightmare only moments later; one of our babies was going to die.

A 'second opinion' scan was scheduled for the following Monday. That weekend was the longest in my life. We had been left with no idea about the prognosis, possible outcome, the choices we may be faced with… nothing. The scan report stated that Twin 2 most likely had a condition called 'holoprosencephaly'. I couldn't even say it, let alone understand its implications.

The emotions that swamped us over the next few days were completely overwhelming. How does one integrate the feeling of grief for one baby with the feeling of joy for the other? After all, we'd only wanted one healthy baby and we still had that. So why did it feel so terrible? I don't know the answer to that question. As an expectant mother, every cell in your body and every thought in your psyche are programmed to creating, and protecting the life that is growing inside you. When you discover that there are two lives instead of one, those feelings are doubled, not halved.

Had I done something wrong? Thankfully I had a clean conscience. I hadn't drunk alcohol, smoked, taken medication and I'd eaten more healthily than I ever thought I could! We had one healthy, developing baby so I knew that it wasn't something I had done. But still I felt inadequate. My job in pregnancy was to provide an environment for our baby to flourish and something somewhere had gone wrong. We would never discover why.

Just a few hours after the appointment, we named the little baby Coran. It means 'heart' to us. We had seen that little baby's heart beating so strong, against all the odds. Despite the fact that we would never get to know who this person was, never know what his or her favourite colour was, never see him or her grow, we knew that we would love that baby for the rest of our lives. So Coran was the right name.

I woke up in tears every day, re-living the shock and the sadness anew each morning. If I woke in the night (as all pregnant women are inclined to do), the thoughts would rush into my mind making sleep practically impossible. Tiredness and pregnancy hormones do not help one deal with such difficult, emotional issues.

As Monday approached, my fears of the unknown grew. Would they keep me in hospital from that point on? Would they suggest an early delivery by caesarean? What would happen when Coran died? Would we have to have invasive tests or maybe even be given the option of a 'selective termination'? These thoughts terrorised me. The not-knowing plagued me. I was preparing myself for the worse.

St George's Hospital in Tooting is an enormous place. We arrived half an hour early and used the time walking the half-mile distance from where we'd finally found a place to park our car to the antenatal department. We booked in at the reception and were asked if we'd attended before. Nobody seemed to know or care that we'd been referred from another hospital. We were told to wait in a large, square, bare room with 6 or 7 other women – some with partners and young children – perched uncomfortably on plastic chairs, like those we used to have at school.

Our name was called three minutes before our allotted appointment time. We were led into a darkened room with a large ultrasound machine by a Doctor with a soft, friendly voice. He asked, "So what can I do for you today?" I couldn't believe that he had to ask. Surely everybody in the world knew that ours had come crashing down around us? Why did he have to ask such a ridiculous question? My logical mind cut in and I answered his question explaining that a scan four days previously had revealed a twin pregnancy with an anomaly in the second foetus.

We had decided over the weekend that we did, after all, want to find out the sex of the bigger baby. There were too many uncertainties now. That moment of birth was not going to be the joyous one we had envisaged; a moment where we delight in the news that we have a baby boy or baby girl. We needed to answer as many of our questions as possible. So we asked the Doctor to tell us if he could see if it was a boy or a girl. It was a girl! 'Ella'. My eyes watered from the joy of the news. It was Jeremy's instincts that had been right on that one! I secretly knew that he'd hoped it was a girl all along.

The Doctor proceeded to carry out a thorough examination of Ella and confirmed the previous opinion that all seemed perfectly well with her. There were no signs of abnormality and she was a good size for her gestational age, with an estimated weight of 482 grams.

The attention was then moved to Coran. The head, femur and abdomen were all measured. The weight was estimated at just 194 grams. For what seemed like an age, the image was left hovering over the little heart beating. Nothing was said. But something seemed wrong. We later read on the scan report that there was 'asymmetry' and an 'abnormal axis' in the heart.

I loved watching that little heart beating. It confirmed that Coran is very much alive. And we saw kicking too! That was a lovely moment. However long or short his or her life is going to be, even if it's just these few weeks, we saw life there. We saw purpose. We saw so much more than a bundle of cells that had failed to develop properly.

Perhaps some souls only need a very short time in order to complete unfinished business. Perhaps the lessons that Coran sought this time round can be learnt in the womb. Perhaps this is just a 'trial run'. Perhaps Coran is too highly evolved spiritually to need a physical life on this planet. Perhaps Coran is Ella's guardian angel and they made a pact before incarnating to stay together in this beginning. We'll never know, of course. But it helps us to believe that there is a bigger plan; one that we'll probably never understand. I find it hard to believe that these things are random. Fate has dealt us this hand and somehow we will deal with it.

It was just three weeks ago that we found out that we had twins. There is still a long way to go. Every day brings uncertainty. Every twinge makes me wonder, "Is this it?" But for now we will leave Mother Nature to have her way. We have no difficult choices to make. There are no tests to be done. It is a waiting game.

Every day is so important. Every day increases Ella's chances of survival should labour start early. And every day is one more day in which we are a family of four.

6ᵗʰ June – Hopes, theories and fantasies

I feel that Coran is a girl. I think she made a pact with Ella to accompany her to the moment of birth. I am no longer afraid that Coran will pass away before the end of the pregnancy; I think she will hang on to the last minute and we will have one precious moment where we will look into her eyes before she moves on. We will honour her life, even though that life only existed inside my own body. For that I feel so privileged. She is so much wiser than me. It is not for me to teach her, as is the normal expectation of a mother. Rather, it is her who is teaching me. She is teaching me to accept what life offers you and to find beauty and peace in the hardest moments. She is teaching me to live in the moment rather than allow one's anxieties to cloud the reality of the present. She is teaching me to open my heart, to unblock my emotions and to feel like I have never felt anything before. She is teaching me to love, respect and cherish those who I have around me, especially her twin sister, Ella, who has had such a special beginning.

I even wonder if perhaps Coran has been around me before. Perhaps she has already tried to teach me all these things but I was unable, or unwilling, to hear her. Only by incarnating in a little body that will never be able to survive outside my womb, was I forced to face the lessons that she is able to teach me. It is hard. It is so very hard. And yet I know now that Coran is my angel. Coran is Ella's angel. Coran is Jeremy's angel. She is already an angel although she continues to live inside me. She will always be remembered. And she will always be in my heart.

9th June – Shock, numbness and fear

I read an article about the different stages of grief after the loss of a multiple. I realise that I have only just come out of the first stage; "Shock and numbness". I had felt detached, that the situation was surreal. There were even days when I was able to carry on as if nothing had happened and perhaps even fool myself with romantic ideologies and philosophies to help me get through. The diagnosis was a concept rather than a reality.

I have now moved into the second stage; "Searching and yearning" in which I am apparently likely to seek out as many facts as I can as well as experience a longing to hold my lost baby in my arms. It is confusing. We haven't lost anybody yet. And yet we know that this will be the outcome. I have tried searching and have found so little. There are a couple of online groups that have been a great source of support – The Centre for Loss in Multiple Births and Loss in Multiple Birth Outreach (eLimbo – one of Yahoo's e-mail groups). It has been good to finally make contact with other women who know what it feels like, even if they are on the other side of the world.

I have also become particularly aware of a very strong anxiety that I have. I think I've been trying to deny it and I feel guilty for feeling it: I'm terrified about how Coran might look when (s)he is born. When I first heard the diagnosis, I had a brief look on the internet for information about her condition (holoprosencephaly) and discovered that it often causes facial deformities including 'cyclopia' when only one eye develops. I thought it would help me to do more research. It didn't at all. On the contrary. It has really scared me. I saw some awful images of babies with various degrees of severity of this condition. Now I'm scared that I'm going to be horrified at the sight of Coran. I feel guilty even admitting it. But it's true and I have to admit and face this fear if I'm going to even attempt to get over it.

I'm hoping that my motherly instinct will help me see past physical appearances and that when I hold Coran in my arms, I will simply see the most beautiful little baby in the world (with the exception perhaps of Ella). But I'm still scared. No-one can comfort me. Only time will tell.

10th June – So much sadness

I feel so sad that Coran will never know Daddy. Coran's inside me, so can feel me, get to know me, share my emotions and be intimately entwined with my spirit. Jeremy can feel Coran kick but can (s)he feel him? I sincerely hope so. It makes me so sad that Coran will never feel the love that Jeremy has for her and will never reap the benefits that would come from being his child.

I feel so sad that I'll never walk in the woods with Coran holding one hand and Ella the other. I feel sad that we'll never buy them matching outfits or watch them fighting over the remote control! It's the simple things that I'm going to miss.

Will every milestone that Ella makes remind me that Coran isn't here to reach them too? How can we celebrate a birthday that will always remind us of our loss? Will I be able to lose myself in pride and happiness when Ella takes her first steps or will that moment only remind me that Coran is not here to ever make a single step?

Perhaps there will always be a conflict between these emotions. Can there ever be resolution when dealing with birth and death in the same instance? There are so many questions.

We saw Mavis at East Surrey Hospital today. She's a midwife who has also trained in counselling. She was lovely and very compassionate and understanding. But it reminded me, once again, that our situation is not 'fixable'. However kind and caring people may be, nobody can take away the hurt or give us back a sorrow-less pregnancy.

I wish that I'll wake up and find that it's all been a terrible dream. I dream that I'll wake up from this nightmare and life will be restored to that of a 'normal' expectant couple. But I know that cannot be.

It is so unfair. Life can be so cruel. Holoprosencephaly has an incidence rate of 1 in 285,714. That's less than a 0.00% chance! So why us? Why me? I have always done my best to be kind, to do the 'right' thing, to seize every opportunity that life presents me. I have never knowingly hurt anyone and am so sorry to anybody that I have hurt accidentally. I have never taken life for granted or forgotten to thank the universe for all that there is to be grateful for. So why has this happened to us? We don't deserve it. Life can be so unfair.

What if there is no higher power or bigger plan? What if we are just a series of biochemical accidents that has somehow led to life and consciousness? What if there is no meaning that one day we'll come to understand? Perhaps these ideas are all delusions after all; delusions that we humans indulge in order to ameliorate the inevitable pain and suffering that accompany life.

I try to stay optimistic and positive. But it is so very hard when every moment is accompanied by shadows. Jeremy does his best to remind me of all that we have to be thankful for. He's a great support. I worry though that he's not allowing his own sadness and grief to surface in order to protect me from them. And how many times can I cry on his shoulder? He's a 'fixer' but he can't fix this. He's learning to be a great listener but I know he's hurting too. Seeing me in pain only adds to his own.

13th June – Managing the pain

I am feeling more positive today. Friday night was the most painful day yet. I cried and cried for five hours and couldn't imagine that it would ever stop. But it finally did around midnight. The pain never goes away. I don't suppose it ever will. Jeremy and I decided that it was going to be rather like managing asthma: The grief will come in particularly bad attacks and will always be underlying the surface. Hopefully with time, the attacks will become less severe and less frequent but each one will be as uncomfortable as the last.

Somehow we got through the weekend. The tears were constantly close and when they fell, they did so silently.

I can tell now who's kicking me! Ella seems to particularly like music with strong rhythms. She's moving around (dancing?) within minutes of an upbeat song playing on the radio and she seems particularly partial to Latin jazz! Coran always wakes up just as Jeremy and I settle down to sleep. It's wonderful because Jeremy can feel Coran kicking now when he places his hand on my belly. It often seems like I feel Coran more than I feel Ella. Perhaps because of her (his?) position or perhaps because, being smaller, (s)he has more room to move around! When they kick me, I tell them I love them. Often they kick me again after that, as if they've heard and understood me. I love those moments. It is only in these moments that exist now that I will be able to interact with our little Coran. I tried to sing them lullabies on Friday but the lyrics 'waking' and 'sleeping' made me too sad knowing that Coran will only ever sleep.

15th June – Longing for tangible pain

I can feel myself nose-diving again. The last few days have been ok but yesterday was plagued by a strange feeling of emptiness and today I woke up and immediately started to cry. I've been thinking about the delivery. In so many ways I feel that a 'natural' delivery is by far the best option for all of us: It's what I've always wanted to experience and I feel that somehow it must be an easier, more gradual passage for the baby rather than just being wrenched out of the womb on a set day at a set time. I also feel that it would give me a chance to fulfil Coran's destiny as nature truly intended. If there is any rhyme or reason to this crazy situation then perhaps it is best to intervene as little as possible.

I've even started to look forward to the pain of childbirth! It is, after all, a tangible pain and so different in that respect to the emotional pain that is engulfing me. I've started to look forward to screaming and shouting… something I've wanted to do since 12th May but have either been unable or unwilling to do. In a way, it feels like the process of natural delivery and the pain that accompanies it might be quite cathartic.

But this morning I had a different thought. Suppose that we attempt a natural delivery and Ella is born first and Coran is still alive. After a few precious moments acquainting myself with my beautiful new daughter, I will then have to deliver another baby knowing that with every contraction, with every push, I am a few moments closer to losing Coran forever. I know that my physical body will not give me any other option, but will I be strong enough emotionally to handle that? I can't even imagine how that will feel. I'll then have to deal with emotional pain at the same time as the physical pain and I honestly don't know how I could survive that. I would, of course, but a part of me would surely die in the process.

In every possible way I long to have just a few moments with Coran after her birth so that I can look into those eyes and see the soul that resides there. But the pain of knowing the ending is so very great. It sometimes feels that it might be easier for me if Coran was to pass away before delivery and I was then to go into labour the next day. That would save me the trauma of delivering a baby that I know will only live moments, if that. And it will save me the trauma of continuing the pregnancy knowing that I am carrying my dead child. There will be trauma and heartbreak each and every way. To look into Coran's eyes would be a magical experience – heartbreaking, but magical – and one that would stay with me forever.

Perhaps it is even more likely that Coran would survive delivery if we were to have an elective caesarean. Perhaps the trauma of childbirth itself would mean that Coran would die during birth. But if we were to have a section, then that trauma would be saved.

The Health Visitor seemed to think that it was highly likely that I would be offered an elective caesarean. She said that East Surrey Hospital tend to 'veer on the side of caution' in such situations and had a very high rate of sections compared to the national average. (I knew this already from some research I did when I first got pregnant.) Had anyone asked me a couple of months ago, I would have insisted that I would fight against a caesarean at all costs. But now I'm not so sure. There are the obvious disadvantages in terms of longer recovery, major surgery, risk of infection, and so on but it is beginning to seem as if there are advantages to me as well as to the babies. If we attempt a natural delivery, I know that even if one of the twins is born successfully, there is a very high likelihood that the second one would need to be born by caesarean. This seems to be a very common outcome in twin pregnancies, even ones without complications such as ours. So if there is such a high probability of that, why not go for an elective caesarean anyway?

These questions are mostly academic at the moment. I'm going to see the new consultant on 13th July – I complained about the first one who was so very uncompassionate and this was the next available appointment. Yet again, I find myself waiting and without any answers to the millions of questions that I have. I suspect there's a reason for that too; it forces me to sort out my emotions before addressing the practical issues with which we're faced (I think my usual tendency is to do things the other way round!)

We have another dilemma to work through too. Our antenatal NCT (National Childbirth Trust) classes are due to start on 30th June. It's a class for six couples, all first-timers, that runs weekly with the last session on 1st September. It's for preparing for natural delivery, birth positions, coping with labour as well as how to look after a newborn and very importantly, meeting other new parents in the area. So Sod's Law would have it that out of the six, there's another couple expecting twins! It's extraordinary the run of extremely unlikely things that have happened to us!

I've just had a flashback to statistics lessons (that also is an extremely unlikely occurrence, I might add!) – if 1 in 100 pregnancies are twins, then out of 6 couples chosen at random, there's only a probability of… nope, actually I can't work it out. That's too challenging for my mushy brain right now! But the odds of there being another couple expecting twins, in a group of just 6 is very, very low. I don't know if I could handle it. On good days, I know that I'll be delighted for them that they have two healthy babies to bring into this world. But how will I feel on the bad days? Will I feel angry? Jealous? Resentful? I truly hope that I would only feel great joy for their good luck but it would kind of be rubbing it in my face and a constant reminder of what we might have had. I really don't know what to do. I keep changing my mind. On Monday I was sure that we'd go to the classes; after all, we'll need more support than we originally thought and we will still be parents of a newborn baby. Today I don't think I could bear to do it. There's also, of course, the issue of whether or not it's worth spending ten weeks preparing for an 'active labour' and 'natural delivery' when I might end up having an elective caesarean anyway.

I wish someone could just tell me all the answers.

17th June – No respite from my troubles

I always look forward to a bit of 'light reading' (!) when the Society of Homeopath's journal arrives. I saw it on the doormat this morning and thought, "A-ha! A cup of tea and half an hour with the journal will be a nice respite from my troubles".

And what did I see when I opened the envelope? A picture of a screaming newborn baby and a title "Birth & Death - homeopathy at the extremes of life".

Extraordinary synchronicity. Who'd have thought it? Why this issue now? I am confronted with our troubles at every corner and every turn. When I try to get away from it, it comes and slaps me in the face and says, "Don't even think about having a break!"

I'll be writing to the Editor with our own story of homeopathy in 'Birth and Death'.

21st June – It'll all turn out for the best

Well I'm delighted to say that the 'nose-dive' I was so sure was coming on a week ago never materialised. I even think that perhaps the homeopathic remedy I took on the 10th has really helped me. I haven't had a 'breakdown' since that terrible Friday. I even feel like I've turned a corner in my grief. I haven't cried today nor did I cry yesterday. In fact, I didn't cry all weekend, much to my surprise. Of course, I still feel desperately sad and far from 'OK' but things feel better and I feel more positive and in touch once again with my belief that somehow – however hard it is to see right now – everything will turn out for the best.

I am anxious though. We have another scan tomorrow. I am concerned that I haven't felt so much movement these last few days (perhaps for four days). I suspect, well hope, that it's just from the heat (it was over 30 degrees today) but I'm worried that Coran has left us. I am trying to put that thought to the back of my mind for now.

Mostly I'm looking forward to seeing our babies and finding out how much they've grown. I am sure that Ella is still doing great and is developing perfectly for her gestational age. I hope that Coran has at least grown a little bit, and perhaps we'll even be able to find out if (s)he's a boy or a girl. It would be good to know. I'm also really looking forward to getting some more scan photos to add to our collection. It's important to me to save as much as possible for our 'memory box' and 'memory book' that I'm planning to make. So many people have written wonderful e-mails and sent us beautiful cards and I want to be able to keep them somewhere to honour Coran's life, however short it may be.

Hopefully the doctors will be able to answer more of our questions too, particularly in relation to how Coran may look at delivery. It's not such an active anxiety as it was a couple of weeks ago, but it's still on my mind.

I re-read the scan report and found something very interesting: Although the initial diagnosis was holoprosencephaly, it seems that there is a query that it may in fact be hydranencephaly. I have researched on the internet and it seems that the two are hard to differentiate from scans. They carry the same prognosis though. In hydranencephaly, the brain's cerebral hemispheres are absent and replaced by sacs filled with cerebrospinal fluid. Again, it will be good to know and I hope they'll be able to tell us more tomorrow.

22nd June – Coran has died

The scan showed that Coran has died. The Doctor thinks it happened some time in the last 2 to 4 days. I feel numb with shock. We were also told that we'll probably never know if Coran is a boy or a girl and what caused his/her death. It's been a very hard day.

23rd June – A tree to watch grow

Mum bought us a beautiful rose plant today of a type called "Happy Child". We will plant it in our garden in memory of Coran. We also bought a tree (a small one – about 7 feet tall) which has beautiful purple, heart-shaped leaves. I'm looking forward to watching it grow.

It's been an odd day; very up and down. It still seems very surreal and almost distant. I don't think I have been able to accept what has happened yet. I am seeing Mavis for some counselling tomorrow. Perhaps that will help me come to terms with it.

I have had some lovely e-mails from the ladies on the eLIMBO e-mail group. It's good to know that there are others out there who have been through, and survived this sort of situation. They are a great source of support. As when we first found out about the twins, our family and friends have all been fantastic. Not a single person has said a 'wrong' thing and I feel so lucky to be surrounded by such lovely people.

Jeremy and I have been thinking hard about when Coran may have died. I am sure that I felt her move on Saturday when we were in Devon – my sisters were trying to feel the kicking. On Sunday morning I remember having strange heart palpitations that took my breath away. That evening we stopped at Stonehenge on the way home. Jeremy, in particular, was very taken with the energy there and we discussed the possibility of scattering Coran's ashes there. We think that Coran died sometime on Sunday, perhaps whilst we were at Stonehenge. So 19th June will be

'Coran's Day'. It will be better for Ella that her birthday will not be shared with a sad day.

I'm exhausted. Not so much physically, but emotionally. Hoping I'll be able to sleep tonight.

24th June – Simmering emotions

I saw Mavis today at the hospital, for counselling. She's a lovely lady – very compassionate and caring. But even in all her experience, she has only seen one other couple who have been through something like this. When I hear how unusual it is, I can't help asking, "Why me?" When I ask it, the situation feels even more surreal, not less.

The counselling was helpful, I think. Perhaps it's too early to tell. Mavis seems to think that I'm still in shock and to properly 'go to' the emotions would be too painful right now. I think she's right. It's as if I get flashes of the true emotions but no sooner are they there on the surface, then they get shoved back down again. It's not intentional; I know the importance of letting out one's feelings, and I'm not purposefully trying to stop them. But they're not quite ready to come up yet. It's as if they're simmering.

I miss Coran. Truly I miss Coran. I miss feeling those little feet kicking under the right side of my ribs. (She was laying transverse so I often felt movements quite high up and right round the side.) I miss feeling kicks on one side followed by kicks on the other side. I miss saying, "I'm taking the twins for a walk" and I miss people saying, "Hello, you three!" I miss telling them in turn how much I love them and how I hope that they don't feel the pain that I'm feeling.

Are there two babies now or just one? There are still two babies inside me, that's for sure. But one of them is not alive. What does that mean? How does one process that? To talk of 'my baby' seems wrong somehow, because we have two. To talk of 'my twins' sounds wrong because one of them isn't with us anymore. In fact, nothing feels right; because nothing is right! This isn't how it is supposed to be.

I'm angry but there's nobody to be angry with. There's nobody I can shout at, shake my fist at or just be plain nasty to! There is no blame to be placed anywhere. No-one is at fault. Nobody could have done anything differently to affect the outcome. Our baby has died and there is no reason. There are no explanations. Perhaps there are a few 'what ifs' but even they would only have momentarily affected the outcome. "What if I hadn't gone to Devon for the weekend and subjected my body and my babies to the long drive in the heat?" The answer is simple. Nothing would be different. Perhaps Coran may have lived another day and I would have felt a few more kicks, but ultimately nothing would be different.

We only knew about Coran's life for six weeks. They are six weeks I will never forget. Six weeks I never want to forget. I want to hold on to them forever and remember every little moment. I will always remember the feeling of elation when we were told that we had twins and the feeling of insurmountable grief when we found out just a few minutes later that one of them was unlikely to survive. I'll always remember the tickle of kicks that were from Coran – mostly when I was lying in bed at night and always on the right side of my body, either just below my ribs or further down, just above my hip. I will always remember saying, "I love you" and being kicked back almost immediately. I am sure that Coran and I connected this way. I miss that. And I will always miss that. I hope that I will always remember.

It has been six weeks that have affected a lifetime.

We have a hard weekend ahead. We have a neighbour's party tomorrow afternoon and are seeing friends tomorrow evening. We have a lunch arranged on Sunday and a BBQ to attend in the evening. How can I tell all those people what has happened? To not tell them is dishonest and dishonourable to Coran's life. I have to tell them. But at what point in the conversation do you tell something like this? I'm very aware that many people don't know what to say or how to react to such news. When that happens, it makes me feel worse, and then everybody feels awkward. Somehow I think I have to forewarn everybody of the news and explain that we may not stay long, that I may need to make myself scarce for a few moments or that I may start crying at any moment. I want to see my friends. I don't want to sit at home wallowing. But it takes courage that perhaps is hard to find right now.

One of the things that I am very relieved about is that I don't feel 'freaked out' knowing that Coran has died but is still inside me. In many ways, it is nice to know that the physical part of her is still with me. I don't want to give that up and the delivery will still be hard, knowing that it will be a final goodbye. We talk so little about death, dying and the dead in our culture and in some ways I feared that it would feel 'freaky' to be carrying my baby's dead body in my tummy. But it doesn't. Coran is my baby and will always be my baby. Any mother wants their baby with them, as I do right now.

I worry about Ella, of course. I worry that I'll go into pre-term labour. I worry that living alongside Coran's body for the next 10 weeks will have an impact on her. I worry that she will grow up feeling that part of her is missing. But mostly I worry that I am not providing her with the best possible environment due to my grief. If it's true that babies pick up their mother's emotions, then Ella has lived a whole lifetime of emotions these last six weeks! (Perhaps Coran did too then…) Something tells me she will be fine. The scan showed that she is still lying in the breech position, bum-down, and the consultant at St George's stated very clearly that if she doesn't shift positions, then they will recommend a Caesarean section at 38 weeks. He said that even though Coran has died, the placenta is still acting as a twin placenta; they tend to deteriorate after 38 weeks, so if I am still going by then, they will either induce or section at this stage. That brings our estimated delivery dated to 2nd September. One day after mine and a day before my mother-in-law's birthday!

There are very high risks now that I will go into labour early. I have to go for steroid injections on Monday and Tuesday (they must be 24 hours apart) to help Ella's lungs develop. I have researched the internet and am happy that there are no adverse side-effects for Ella. And I will do anything to improve her chances in case she comes early. The midwife said today that if we get to 32 or 33 weeks, then her chances for survival are very good. That's just another five weeks away. I am taking one day at a time but if we can get to the end of July, I will be able to breathe a slight sigh of relief.

28th June – Safety and comfort in our own home

I haven't written for a few days. They've been odd ones. We ended up cancelling all our social commitments for last weekend; I just couldn't face them. Everybody has been very understanding and it was right to have some time in the safety and comfort of our own home.

Sunday was the reality check that I'd been waiting for. Ella started to kick me on the right hand side on Saturday evening. It reminded me so much of how Coran used to feel. Then Julie, the midwife, came round on Sunday. Nobody had told her of our news, so that was the first hard thing. She was great and gave me a lovely, big cuddle. But it was extremely difficult to hear just the one heartbeat. I think some silly, irrational, hopeful part of me had come to believe that it had been Coran kicking me and that perhaps the scan at St George's had been wrong. So to hear just one heartbeat confirmed the news. It's so sad. So very, very sad.

When Julie left, I burst into tears and couldn't stop for over an hour. I find that I can be so strong when other people are around but that as soon as it is just Jeremy and I, the floodgates spill open. He's the only one that I can really cry with. I don't mean to stop the tears when I'm with other people, but for some reason they just don't come, or if they do, they come silently. There is a barrier up that I can't break down. I'm not sure where it comes from or why it is there, but I always seem able to put on a brave face when others are around. I suppose that's a good thing. I can't go blubbering all over every person I see!

The steroid injections have been pretty harrowing. It's not the procedure itself that's bad, but the to-ing and fro-ing from the hospital and, once again the reality of the situation. The injections themselves were far from pleasant! Not painful, but definitely uncomfortable and they left me with a numb-bum for an hour or so on both occasions! I had to do it though, for Ella's sake. I'll do anything for her.

I was an hour late for the appointment today. Mavis, who administered the injections, was extremely understanding. I'd not had a good night's sleep; I'd been thinking about the possibility of having a 3D scan to see if there's any chance we can get a photographic image of Coran, before his or her little body deteriorates too much. We just don't know what we'll be left with by the time of delivery. Time is obviously of the essence so I felt that it was important to make a decision quickly. And decisions are so very hard right now anyway! I'd written to a couple of clinics over the weekend and saw a reply from one of them late last night saying that they could fit me in on Wednesday at midday. So I had to make a quick decision.

When I got to my parents' this morning (Mum has been great and accompanied me to the hospital on the last few occasions) I started discussing the possibility of the scan with Mum and Dad. A whole gamut of emotions came out and holding myself together was no longer an option. It was a very hard decision to make. On the one hand, it may be that we won't be able to get a picture at all, in which case the journey into London and £200 would be wasted, not to mention all the unnecessary stress. Or it might be that we get a picture that is very harrowing and maybe even disturbing. On the other hand, we might get just the picture we want so that we have something material to remember Coran by. It's just so very hard not knowing who this little person is!

Ultimately, I decided that I would have the scan. At the very least, we'll get a lovely 3D picture of our Ella, which we will treasure like everything else. I can always decide not to look at the photos of Coran if it's too hard to do so. But if I don't have it, I can never go back or have it done at a later date. It's really now or never. I don't want to have any regrets. I don't want to ever think "If only…" It's going to be a very hard day and a difficult experience: To see images of our little babies – one alive and kicking and the other still, but hopefully peaceful. But it must be done. Unfortunately, Jeremy can't come due to work commitments, but we'll get a DVD so he can see the whole thing.

I've also been thinking (and worrying) a lot about the birth again. I've realised that I'm terrified of it. Before we knew about these complications, I was really looking forward to a home birth. I was looking forward to feeling the power of ultimate womanhood and bringing my baby into the world surrounded by calm, love and home. Love will still be there, but calm and home are now out of the question. There will also be the added emotions of grief and fear, which I wish so much I didn't have to subject her little self to at all, least of all in her first few moments.

If Ella turns round, so that she is head-down, I hope that she decides to come before 38 weeks is up (before 2nd September). I really can't stand the thought of an induced labour, with all the monitoring and drugs that it involves. If she hasn't turned, and remains in the breech position, then it will be a caesarean section with all the fear and worry that brings with it. (Not to mention the six weeks of not driving, the risks of infection, the increased risks of breathing difficulties in babies born by C-section, and so on.) I keep having to remind myself that what will be, will be, and that worrying about it now won't help in any way.

Physically, I'm definitely feeling heavy these days. Getting in and out of Jeremy's MG is quite a challenge now! (It's going on the market soon; it's time to get a grown-up car!) I weighed myself this evening and was shocked to discover that I weigh the best part of 13 stone! And I measured my belly – 43 inches all the way round! I guess Ella is having a growth spurt. At her gestational age, she'll be laying down layers of fat under her skin now. She's opening and closing her eyes, responding to light and touch stimuli and getting into regular patterns of sleep. She's preparing to be born! But she must stay in there at least another six weeks, and hopefully ten. She's a fighter and she's strong. I just can't wait to meet her.

1st July – Seeing the babies

So much seems to have happened in the last three days. I'm feeling stronger today though, so it feels right to write again.

I went for the scan on Wednesday. I was terribly nervous, jittery, scared, sad, excited… you name it, I was feeling it! In my typical Virgoan fashion, I insisted that we arrived there twenty minutes early, only to be kept waiting for half an hour after my allotted appointment time. Not nice when I was so very anxious. I got to see Professor Stuart Campbell, the pioneer of the 3D/4D scanning technology, so I knew from the outset that we had the best chances of getting photos of the babies, even if there was still a possibility that we'd get nothing. We didn't get any pictures of Coran's face, but we got so much more than nothing.

Unfortunately, Coran was turned away (facing my back) so it wasn't possible to see her from the front. But I saw her little, tiny body. The Professor estimated that she's probably only about 15 centimetres long, and weighs just over 200 grams. That's really tiny. She has already got smaller but he reckons that she won't get that much smaller over the next few weeks. She is lying up under my right ribs, all curled up. It wasn't possible to determine her gender, but it was interesting that the Professor kept referring to Coran as 'she', even though I didn't!

The most incredible thing was seeing pictures of Ella. She's beautiful, of course! The extraordinary thing is that she is curled right up next to Coran. The Professor tried on several occasions to get a clear picture of Ella's face and in every single one, you can see Coran's body just to the right side of Ella's face. It's beautiful. They are continuing to look after each other in there.

The experience was traumatic, emotional, exhausting but well worthwhile. I know now that I won't ever wonder, "If only…" and for that, it was worth it. We have the whole hour long session on DVD, so although Jeremy was unable to come, he was able to see his babies on the screen.

Yesterday was horrible. I woke up at 5am with pains in my abdomen; scary for any pregnant woman but especially when I am so aware of our risks now. I tried for an hour or so to get back to sleep but the pains kept coming. I didn't think it was contractions – they seemed too high for that – but I was worried nevertheless. The main focus of the pain was in the area that Coran is lying. After a while, I got up and had some breakfast, hoping that would help, but there was no change. I then had a lukewarm bath, but again no change. I felt rotten with it too; feverish and thirsty with a really dry mouth. At 8:30 am I phoned the midwife, Julie, who suggested that I go to the hospital to be checked out. She thought that it probably wasn't pre-term labour but that I may have an infection of some sorts that should be investigated anyway.

My darling husband phoned work and told them the news and off we set. Whilst we were in the car, the pain changed location. It moved down to my lower abdomen. But still it wasn't cramping. It was as if there was a ball in my abdomen that was being alternately blown up and let down. I don't think it's even right to call it painful, but it was certainly very uncomfortable.

The hospital midwives and doctors were great, as always. There were leukocytes in my urine, suggesting an infection of some sorts, although I didn't have a temperature. I was hooked up to the monitor for twenty minutes and Ella's little heartbeat was perfectly fine. There was no 'uterine activity' so I wasn't having contractions.

It was a relief, but to a part of me also a disappointment. I am just exhausted. The burden that I am carrying is just too heavy for me. Knowing that little Coran has died but that I must go on for Ella is an impossible situation. I simply don't know where I am going to find the strength. So a part of me was secretly hoping that perhaps I'd deliver early. Ella has a good chance of surviving now although I know that another few weeks could make all the difference to her. I was also secretly hoping that they might decide to keep me in 'for observation'. There is a part of me that would like to relinquish all responsibility and if I were in hospital, I wouldn't have to constantly make the judgement of "This is normal" or "This needs to be checked out"; I could just surrender myself to the experts and sleep.

I am so tired. I am completely drained of energy. In the bad moments, I also find that I have lost all enthusiasm and even hope. I imagine the worst things happening to Ella. It is as if I can no longer trust that anything will go right. How can I when so much has gone wrong? I try to remind myself that 'right' and 'wrong' are small, human judgements to make and that somehow this situation is perfect in exactly the way that it is. This was how it was meant to be, and this is how it is. But when I'm hurting, it's so hard to stay in touch with that. I feel empty. Sometimes it is as if there is nothing left at all. I don't know where I'll find the strength to go on for another 9 weeks, which I hope I can do, for Ella's sake. I have framed a photo of her from the scan – with Coran at her side – to remind me of why I must go on. I don't want to let her down but I feel like I do every moment when I feel sad or anguish or hopelessness. She is so important to me and I want the best for her.

Since finding out about the twins, every emotion I have has two sides. When I feel happy, it reminds me of the sadness. When I feel excitement, it comes with fear. When I feel grateful for the beauty that is growing inside me, I feel anger and pain for the loss of my other child. Nothing is simple anymore. It never will be again.

9th July – Existing despite the pain

I have coped this week. On Monday morning, I didn't know how I would. I had no appointments booked and no milestones to reach that would help me measure the time. But in some way, that has helped. It has helped me to get back to some sense of normality. It's not really normality, of course, but it's a few notches further away from being consumed and drowned in the feelings of grief, sadness and fear. So I have been able to focus on some work, I was able to find excitement in helping my sister buy a car, I was able to enjoy Jeremy's birthday – I have rediscovered myself in some ways. I have found that I do still exist amongst the turmoil.

It has had a dangerous side too though – I think I have been somewhat detached. At times last week I even felt like I wasn't pregnant. I found myself running up the stairs! I bent down to pick something up and found it easy! My bump hasn't even felt so big. In fact, I measured my bump and it is an inch smaller than when I last measured it two weeks ago – 42 inches round now. This worries me, of course, so I have booked a scan on Wednesday to check that everything is OK with Ella. I suspect that the fluid around Coran has now dissipated so that Ella is growing into that space rather than needing 'new' space but for my peace of mind, I need to know that she is continuing to grow well.

I talked yesterday with Mavis, the counsellor, about these feelings. I was able to pinpoint the problem and actually have been aware of it for some time: When I allow myself to fully feel the joy of being pregnant, to focus on doing the best for my little one, to imagine how wonderful things will be when she is born, I am just reminded of the sadness of our loss and how things *could* have been. So to not feel one allows me the freedom to not feel the other. It doesn't mean that I love or want Ella any less. On the contrary – I love her more than ever and every day I feel the desire to be with her more powerfully than the day before. But as that feeling intensifies and grows, its opposite gets even more painful; I cannot feel one without the other. To protect myself from the pain I also have to protect myself from the joy. This is not a conscious decision, of course, but rather a strategy that the 'survivor' part of my personality has put in place in order for me to cope with the next few weeks.

I don't want to be detached though. I want to feel the joy even if that means that I have to feel the sadness too. But it hurts so much and is so wearying that to have some brief respite from it is a relief.

The respite lasted until yesterday morning. My dear friend, Mary, had very kindly agreed to meet the hospital Chaplain with me so that we could talk about the possibilities for Coran, once the twins have been born. He was a very lovely man; very softly spoken, compassionate and understanding. We discovered that it wouldn't be possible to have a cremation and service in the hospital (the hospital simply doesn't have that facility). The only place in the hospital that we could have a service, with Coran present, would be the mortuary, which is not at all what we wanted. We also won't be able to have a burial or a cremation until we have registered the stillbirth and got a certificate from the Registry Office. (It's so horrid that there is red tape and bureaucracy to deal with in such a situation.) So there will most likely be at least a week between birth and burial. It's even more waiting for closure.

After seeing the Chaplain and having my appointment with Mavis, Mary and I went to the Surrey and Sussex crematorium. It was beautiful. It was perfect. It is set amongst great big, old trees and the air is clean and full of life. All around the crematorium and chapel are memorial gardens where people have dedicated roses, acers, rhododendrons and other beautiful plants and shrubs to their lost loved ones. There is an enclosed garden, "Farthing Wood", which is dedicated especially to babies who were born still. There are maybe 15 or 20 memorials in there. There are memorial plaques with beautiful poems inscribed on them; parents have placed toys and angel statues; siblings have left birthday cards and drawn pictures for their missing brothers and sisters. It is a perfect place for us to lay Coran's ashes and to have a memorial stone there. As soon as I walked through the arch that led into the garden, the tears started to fall. Mostly the tears were of sadness but a few were of happiness and relief that I had found a place that I could visit forever more in memory of Coran. The only thing missing from the Farthing Wood garden is a bench but it has crossed my mind that perhaps we'll be able to dedicate a bench in Coran's memory so that other parents and families will have a spot where they can rest and reflect whilst remembering their lost little ones.

Mary is going to contact the crematorium and find out about the practical sides of things; the cost of a cremation, how we go about getting a plot in the memorial garden and any other practicalities about which we have not yet thought. But I feel that we have an idea now of what we want. We will have a naming and blessing in the hospital, by the hospital chaplain, with just our little family present – Jeremy, me, Ella and Coran. Then a week or so later we will have a service at the crematorium and a cremation, which friends, family and perhaps even some of the hospital staff can attend if they wish. We have found an 'acorn casket', which we will use either for Coran's ashes or perhaps for her body. An acorn is tiny thing that has the potential for greatness. And yet it is beautiful and perfect in its own right. That is like Coran.

Both the chaplain and Mavis advised me that it may not be a good idea to have our ideas set in stone, since we will not know how we will feel after the birth of the babies. That is true – we cannot possibly know how we will feel – but I do know that I never want to feel in the future a, "What if…" or an, "If only…". To have something in place, if not set in stone, will ensure that we will do what we want, despite how we may feel in the acute situation immediately after the birth.

It's so hard to be thinking about and organising a funeral when most expectant mums are only thinking about and planning for a birth. But it has to be done. We will honour our child's short life and we will always remember how wonderful it was to know Coran.

I found this quote by William Wordsworth that so completely sums up how I feel, ""*I loved the Boy with the utmost love of which my soul is capable; and he is taken from me – yet in the agony of my spirit in surrendering such a treasure I feel a thousand times richer than if I had never possessed it.*" He wrote it in 1812 after the death of his son, Thomas. I know exactly what he means.

11th July – Yin and Yang; Moon and Sun

I had my bump painted yesterday! It was Mary's fab idea. A friend of hers, Sylvie, is a professional make-up artist and had the wonderful inspiration of doing a yin/yang sign on my belly with the Sun and Moon entwined in the symbol. It was so perfect. The names 'Coran' and 'Ella' are both derived from the word 'moon' in different languages (although we didn't know this when we chose the names) and it felt so right to do something that was about twos and doubles.

The Sun and Moon represent the cycle of life and death for me; the inescapable fact that things change, that darkness follows light, which is followed again by darkness. The only thing that we can be absolutely sure of in life is that things won't stay as they are. We live in a universe that is constantly changing and we never know what awaits us around the corner. That is how it is supposed to be. Life is dynamic. Life is a process. And part of that process is death. The Sun and Moon are the symbols of male and female, of the god and the goddess and they are two heavenly bodies that drive and dictate our way of life, even if we have become detached from that reality with our modern existence.

It was wonderful to be able to feel joy in being pregnant. I haven't felt that for so very many weeks. I don't have photos of me pregnant since we found out about the twins – it's been too hard to pose for them! But yesterday I felt proud of my bump. For two hours my bump was nurtured and stroked with make-up brushes in the company of my dearest friends, Mary and Ana. I felt really special. I was able to once again get in touch with the feeling that pregnancy is the ultimate female experience. Despite what has happened, I have still brought life into this world. Despite Coran's death, she was able to experience life for 27 weeks. Despite my fears about Ella, she is alive and kicking and I know in my heart of hearts that she will be beautiful, wise and a blessing to my life.

Appropriately, Ana had bought Jeremy an "I'm the Daddy!" T-shirt for his birthday last week. He wore that as we posed for photos. It was such fun. I felt so happy. I haven't felt that for so long. If (when?) I feel down again over the next weeks, I'll be able to look at the photos of my beautiful, painted bump and re-connect with the joy that I felt yesterday.

14th July – The best thing that ever happened?

We had the long-awaited appointment with the consultant yesterday. I hadn't realised how anxious I was about the appointment until Tuesday evening when all my 'old' feelings of panic and not-knowing re-surfaced. I was still tossing and turning at 2am with 'worst case' and 'best case' scenarios flying through my head. It is strange how I have this tendency to panic that so often accompanies 'not-knowing'.

I needn't have worried. We had a scan before the appointment, which showed that Ella is still breech (bother) but doing fine. Her growth rate seems to have slowed slightly, but all her measurements are within 'normal' range so we have been assured that we needn't be concerned. The scan showed that Coran is continuing to get smaller. (S)he's really very little. But don't the best things come in tiny little packages? Perhaps. Coran is still tucked up under my ribs on the right side.

We talked with the consultant at some length about the options for delivery. It appears that the fact that we have twins is not at all a factor in deciding the best course of action and that it will depend entirely on whether or not Ella turns. If she doesn't, they will recommend an elective caesarean. If she does, we'll attempt a natural delivery. I feel OK about that now. Although I know that I will also have to deliver Coran, our first antenatal class on Tuesday evening helped me get back in touch with my knowledge that birth is not an illness, but a very natural process, which can be a wonderful experience. Thoughts of a natural delivery are still slightly over-shadowed by the fact that if Ella doesn't come spontaneously before 38 weeks, I will be induced, which I am far from keen on. But I guess that's better than a caesarean.

The consultant does not want me to go past 38 weeks due to the fact that the placenta is still functioning as a twin placenta, which tends to deteriorate earlier than in a singleton pregnancy. That's the physical argument anyhow. I also think he recognises that each day is hard for us psychologically and that in many ways, the earlier the better. It's good though to know that there is a maximum of 7 more weeks to wait in this limbo period. It doesn't seem like a long time away at all!

My Mum reminded me that my sisters and I were all born early. So I'm hoping that I have those same genes! The best case scenario is that Ella turns around and comes on her own at about 37 weeks. Fingers crossed!

I was thinking recently again about why this has happened to us. I have generally tried to avoid this question, but every now and again it creeps up on me. I believe in karma; that we 'sow what we shall reap'; that 'what goes around comes around'. What did I do in this life or the last that was so very terrible to cause me to suffer through this awful situation? Is it really something that I deserve? But then I thought that this argument only stands up if this situation really is 'awful'. Perhaps this will turn out to be the best thing that ever happened to me. It has already changed the way that I think, feel and view the world and there may be great things that will come out of it further down the road. Although I am suffering now, suffering is not necessarily a bad thing if good comes out of it and if we grow because of it. I guess it could even be argued that we should be thankful for suffering if it allows us a new perspective on life. Perhaps that's just wishful thinking but it's helping me for now!

19th July – Expecting twins, but only one baby

It's one month to the day since Coran died. It's one month and a day since I felt her move inside me. I feel sad; of course I do. But I know that Coran will always be with us in some way. Certainly she'll be with us in our memories. We made her – she is part me and part Jeremy – so wherever she is, we will be also. Coran will always be a part of Ella, as Ella will always be a part of Coran. I hope that I will be able to feel her soul around us and I hope that Ella will have a sense of Coran's presence as she grows up. Perhaps, in many years' time, when we have healed, Coran will come back to us in the form of another baby. I hope so. I want to have the opportunity to get to know her; an opportunity that we have been denied this time round.

The truth is, I don't want a part of me to be with Coran. I want Coran to be with us. I can persuade myself that everything happens for a reason, but I don't want a reason; I want Coran. I can try to find the lessons that are hidden in the pain, but I don't want a lesson; I want my baby. However much I try to accept the situation – and in a large part, I have been able to do so – the pain is still there. The troughs are less frequent and less deep, but they still hurt like Hell when I'm in them. And I'm in one now.

We had our second antenatal class this evening. It was taken by a 'women's health physiotherapist'. It was useful and helpful in terms of relaxation exercises, labour positions, things that Jeremy can do to help now and during labour, and so on, but we had a surprise. Half way through, the lady asked, "Are you all expecting just one baby?" I didn't know want to say. I was stunned into silence. So I said nothing. Jeremy stayed quiet too. I wanted to shout out, "No! We're expecting twins!" but I knew if I did, I would either have to explain our situation or lie by not explaining more. But I felt I'd lied anyway by not telling the whole truth. It was horrible. My heart was pounding in my chest and my palms went sweaty. I felt so uncomfortable. Then I could feel the tears start to well-up and I only just managed to stop them flowing. Because we are expecting twins; but only one live baby. That's not an easy thing to explain to a group of 10 expectant mums and their other halves.

It totally shook me off balance. I couldn't really concentrate for the rest of the evening and kept finding that I'd drifted off and had missed what the physio was saying. At the same time, there was a model of a pregnant lady – 'cut' in half so you could see the lie of the baby in her womb. I kept looking at it and imagining how different it must be in my own tummy, with Coran lying completely still and all curled up whilst Ella grows and kicks around her! And wow did Ella kick this evening! I had my arms resting on my bump and my arms kept jumping as Ella kicked and punched beneath them!

When I think about the delivery (which antenatal classes obviously make you do), I have all sorts of fears and anxieties to contend with. I think of delivering Ella whilst I'm on all fours and then I have images of Coran just slipping out unexpectedly and landing on the floor. That would be just awful. Or I imagine that Ella will come out holding onto Coran. I know intellectually that these sorts of things are unlikely, if not impossible, but the worry is still there nevertheless. Perhaps it won't be so bad after all if Ella stays breech and I have to have a caesarean. As I'm increasingly having to come to terms with, only time will tell.

22ⁿᵈ July – My belly is flat

I don't know why this week has been so much harder than the last couple. Perhaps it was that experience at the antenatal class. Perhaps it's because each day brings us closer to 'D-Day' and so as I think more about the delivery and how I will cope with saying hello to Ella whilst saying goodbye to Coran, it gets harder and harder.

I have had some strange experiences this week too. Every morning for the last 7 and a half months, I have instinctively touched my belly as soon as I wake up. In the last couple of days, I have touched my belly and found it to be flat. Of course, it's not really flat – when I look, I can see my bump. But in those few moments, it feels flat. I guess it's an expression of the loss and my fear of further loss. It's horrible, absolutely horrible. It's a nasty way to start each day. It helps if Ella kicks or wriggles within the next few minutes (she tends to have a bit of a wiggle when I wake up), but it doesn't take away the fright that I get on feeling a flat tummy. It's very strange.

I've also continued to have pains in my tummy of varying intensity, at any time of day and night. Sometimes they stop me sleeping. They still tend to be focussed over the area where Coran is lying, so I suspect they're psychosomatic. Certainly the midwife doesn't feel that they are anything to worry about.

Sometimes it seems that Ella is lying right on top of where Coran is. That's another horrid feeling. It conjures up images of Coran getting squashed up in there. I know that that can't hurt her now, but the image of it is still disturbing. And poor Ella – I hope she's not feeling squashed up. I hope it's not bad for her. I know that she won't be feeling fear in the same way that I am but I still worry about her.

Jeremy and I have decided that it's important for us to have a 'birth plan' in place. We recognise that the actual delivery is likely to be far removed from our original plan of a natural, active labour and delivery but in a way, it is more important for us now to think about what will happen afterwards. We need to have some idea of how we want to say goodbye to Coran. We have already decided that it would be better for us in the long-term to face any difficult situations now, rather than look back in years to come and have regrets. So we know it will be extremely hard to see and hold Coran, but if we don't, we may regret it forever.

Some people tell us that it will be too hard and it's better that the midwives just take Coran away and leave us to focus on Ella. But then I can imagine that when we look back at this period, it will seem almost surreal. However hard it will be, we want to have photos taken with Coran and keep as much of Coran as we possibly can. Those few moments, possibly hours, after birth, will be the only time that we have.

I feel a bit lost. I feel that I have gone into myself during this last week. There's only so many times that you can discuss the same feelings and I know that nothing anybody says or does can make it feel better. So I think I've started to just 'cope' on my own and 'get on with it'. I think it worked for a while but now it's catching up with me. I had a week or two where I found some degree of normalcy in life again – I returned to work as usual, started cooking proper meals again, even had some good, fun evenings with friends and a silly 'normal' argument with Jeremy! But it was a delusion; because things aren't normal. Everything is still in turmoil.

I'm 32 weeks pregnant today. That means there's a maximum of 6 more weeks to deal with this. Then we can meet our babies, say goodbye to one and concentrate on getting to know the other. Then perhaps we can move onto the next stage.

27th July – I'm a stuck record

I'm beginning to feel a bit like a 'stuck record'. Things just aren't moving forward. Although the intensity of the feelings varies, I feel the same from one day to the next. I can neither move on nor leave these feelings behind. It's very tiring.

Mum and I went to Glastonbury on Monday. The main purpose of the visit was to meet the jeweller who made the beautiful rose quartz heart pendant that I have worn since my Mum bought it for me a few months ago. I have worn it every day since; it is a heart shape, which of course signifies Coran to me and it has a moonstone set in the centre of it. Since the names 'Coran' and 'Ella' are both derivative of the word 'moon' in at least one language, this seems to add extra meaning to the necklace. I decided several weeks ago that it would be lovely to get little versions of the necklace made – one for each of the twins. Louis, the jewellery designer, was very helpful and has made two beautiful little rose quartz hearts, set in silver. They are hand made and therefore totally unique – I even know which one will go to each twin. For now, I am wearing them on my necklace; one on either side of the bigger heart. After they are born, I hope to get photos with Ella wearing hers and the other on a ribbon wrapped around Coran's body. We will keep Ella's for her to wear when she is older and I will keep Coran's as a reminder, in the knowledge that it was always meant for her and that she wore it, albeit briefly.

Glastonbury is a lovely town. My favourite place was the 'Chalice Well Peace Garden'; an extremely peaceful and beautifully designed garden around a natural spring, which has been in use as a 'holy well' for longer than any other well in Europe. It is renowned for being a place where the 'veil between the worlds is thinnest' and I found I could really feel the power of the place. It was beautiful. And Ella seemed to like it too! She wriggled around all day! We sat in the garden and reflected and drank the water directly from the ground. It was delicious! Cool, and as fresh as it comes!

On the way there, I had explained to Mum how surprised I'd been that I hadn't seen a single other tree like the one that we bought the day after we found out Coran had died (it's called a 'Forest Pansy'). The extraordinary thing was that there were two such trees in the Peace Garden! It felt lovely – as if Coran was there somehow, at least in spirit.

On our way back home, we went via Avebury and visited the extraordinary stone circles there. They pre-date the building of Stonehenge and are awesome in a totally different way. Whereas Stonehenge is very structured and complete, the stones at Avebury vary much more in size and shape; they're less chiselled and 'manicured'. It would have been nice to have stayed longer, but it was an appropriate end to our short trip. Unfortunately, we couldn't linger because I had to be back for an antenatal class at the hospital.

The class was horrible. Jeremy is away on work so couldn't come. Mum agreed to come along with me, which was great – it would have been even worse if I'd been on my own. Nothing specifically 'bad' happened. It is just so hard to be in a room full of happy, expectant mums who are experiencing joy in uncomplicated, singleton pregnancies. I haven't told the group about our situation and don't feel that it would be appropriate to: The classes are always very rushed and there's no time set aside for getting to know one another or sharing experiences. The class was taken by the same lady as before. Most regrettably, she had forgotten about our situation. At least, when reminded, she said that she'd remembered the situation but not that my face went with it! So that shook me a bit. And then with everything that is said and with every new topic that is covered, I have a million questions come to mind. I can't ask them because my situation is so unique and it wouldn't be fair on the rest of the group. Even if I did ask the questions, it is unlikely that she'd know the answers anyway. It reminds me of how much I wanted to be pregnant and feel the joy of this wonderful state of womanhood and yet I seem to be so far away from that place where I'd hoped to be.

I was grumpy after the class. I couldn't put my finger on what was wrong, but something had shaken me up. I felt angry. On the drive home I had to stop a couple of times because the tears started to come and wouldn't be held back any longer. I was sad that Jeremy wasn't at home to give me a big cuddle; being without him really made me realise how much I've come to rely on him for support and comfort. Thankfully I had a good night's sleep so I felt a bit better this morning.

Our next appointment with the consultant is a week today. We have a scan beforehand so will find out whether or not Ella has turned around or whether she's remaining stubbornly breech! I have totally come to terms with the prospect of having a caesarean. East Surrey Hospital has a very high rate of caesarean sections (as much as 30%) and although I was horrified when I first read the statistics, I guess it will probably turn out to be to my advantage; at least they are well practised at the procedure! My only concern now is getting through the next 5½ weeks. In one way it feels like no time at all, and it is wonderful to know that five weeks on Friday I will be holding our little girl in my arms. But in another way, it feels like this situation is never-ending and to endure another 37 days seems almost impossible. One way or another, I will do what I have to do.

3rd August – She's growing perfectly

We had a scan and saw the consultant obstetrician at the hospital today. The absolutely fantastic news is that Ella is growing perfectly (her measurements are above average for her dates) and she is estimated to weigh 2.5 kilos – that's 5 pounds 8 ounces! We're so happy that she's doing so well, especially due to my recent worries about my belly not growing! The other great bit of news – I think – is that she's turned over and is now lying head-down.

Why do I hesitate that her positioning is good news? Because I'd totally got used to the idea of having a caesarean and had managed to persuade myself that not only would it be 'OK' but that it would be preferable. We are going to have to deal with so many harrowing and conflicting emotions after the delivery, that there is something appealing about having an elective caesarean, on a fixed date that will be over in less than an hour. The alternative of enduring a potentially long, possibly induced, 'natural' delivery (that may well end in a c-section anyway) and consequently being exhausted and possibly traumatised, does now not seem such a good idea! We are going to need all our strength to give Ella the welcome she deserves whilst enduring the agony of saying 'hello' and 'goodbye' to Coran in the same moment. I feel like I'd have more of that energy available if I had a caesarean.

An induced labour seems to me to be so far from 'natural'. The process will be controlled by drugs, I'll be hooked up to an IV drip, a foetal heart monitor will be strapped to my belly and I will therefore be confined to the bed. It won't be the active, empowering labour and delivery that I had envisaged. And what if something goes wrong?

What if I hear Ella's heartbeat start to fall or rise dramatically? The midwives may know that such a reaction is 'normal' but after what we've been through, I can only imagine the fear that such a situation might bring me. To imagine the prospect of Ella getting distressed during delivery is unbearable. All of these things led me to believe that perhaps a caesarean section would be the best option for delivery after all.

However, the consultant had other ideas. Given that Ella has grown so well and is in such a good position, he is now quite happy to leave things to nature. He said that biologically this would be the best thing to do, although he recognised that what is best for me psychologically may be at odds with this. I am now so confused. And even angry. I feel that each time I get my head around one scenario, everything changes: Just as I manage to come to terms with a particular outcome, the goalposts change and I'm flung back to square one. Jeremy has said the same thing; he has been reading up on caesareans and finding out the best way to support me through it and now he has to go back again to the original 'plan' of a natural delivery! It's hard for both of us.

In many ways I don't even see the point of the antenatal appointments. All I feel I've ever been told is, "We'll have to wait and see!" I understand that birth is far from being an exact science but it would be so good to have at least one certainty in this situation – the method of delivery seems like an obvious choice. It feels like nobody has any idea about the probable outcome but that we'll all just muddle through together somehow. I feel I've been doing that for the last 13 weeks, and I'm tired of it. I'm exhausted and fed up with it.

It's been such a tough week for me. The weekend was particularly difficult. Jeremy was away on work last week so I think I put on a brave face, knowing that he wasn't there to pick me up if I got down. When he got home, all that I'd kept inside came flooding out. On Sunday, I just couldn't stop crying. I woke up a couple of hours earlier than usual yesterday and by 8 am, I was despairing about how I would get through the rest of the day. To have to live through those extra two hours seemed impossible. Thankfully, mum came to the rescue and came over to be with me and I felt much better by the evening. Today I felt stronger and by late afternoon I even felt some connection again with the knowledge that it is best for Ella to stay where she is for as long as possible and that I would be able to bear it for her sake. Yesterday, I thought I would be begging the consultant to deliver the babies at the earliest possible time, preferably next week! It is so up and down. My feelings are so inconsistent. I guess the only thing that any of us can ever be sure of is that things will change! That's truer now than I've ever realised before.

After we saw the consultant, we met up with the hospital Chaplain. We have decided to leave the cremation arrangements to the hospital. It seems simpler that way. We can be involved as much or as little as we wish. I spoke to the Chaplain about my Dad conducting the service, and he assured me that it would be perfectly acceptable and appropriate. He also gave us the necessary stillbirth documentation that we will have to complete after the delivery. It was hard to look through it and know the decisions that we'll have to make. The hospital has a 'baby memorial' book that is kept in the Chapel; it names all the babies that die during pregnancy or soon after delivery. They also hold a memorial service every year at which they read out the babies' names. It's nice that they do that.

Afterwards, Mavis took us to the delivery suite to get familiarised with the room in which I'll most likely have the babies. She knows that we were struggling in our minds with what we would like to happen with Coran after the delivery and she hoped that by familiarising ourselves with the environment we'll be in, that perhaps we'll be able to picture the event more easily and work out what we want. It didn't make it any easier. But perhaps over the next few days we'll figure it out. We're not sure whether we want some time with Ella initially and then want to see and hold Coran, or whether we want to see Coran immediately after the birth. It's a hard one to call. Perhaps we just won't know until the day.

I am now hoping and praying that Ella comes of her own accord before I am induced at 38 weeks. There's quite a high chance of it, given that it's still a twin pregnancy (that tend to deliver early) and that my sisters and I were all born 2-3 weeks early (hopefully I'll take after my mum!). If I go into labour spontaneously, there is at least a possibility that I'll have the type of labour and delivery that I know I really want – natural and with minimum intervention. Surely it's time that we had just a little bit of luck?

15th August – At peace

I can't believe I haven't written in this 'journal' for nearly two weeks! It's testimony in many ways to the fact that I've been feeling OK about things and generally much more at peace with our situation. I think now that the excitement and anticipation of meeting Ella and moving onto the next stage in our parenthood is out-weighing the sadder emotions. Of course, I still feel sad, but I don't cry so often. I can talk and think about Coran without crying every time now. Sometimes, I feel bad about that. It is as if I have become so accustomed to expressing my emotions for Coran through tears and sadness, that if I don't feel it in that way, I worry that I'm not feeling it at all. I'm not sure if that makes sense. I guess the sadness and the grieving became familiar and in some way a reflection of my love for our angel. As those feelings become less acute, I sometimes feel bad that perhaps it is a reflection of the love diminishing. I know in my heart that it doesn't mean that and that Coran would wish us to find hope and joy in what the future holds for us. I have re-found both of those things recently.

I had a worrying dream the other night, which I think brought me in contact with this guilty feeling; I dreamt that I had forgotten Coran's name and I had to ask Jeremy what it was. It was awful. It was as if I was betraying her memory. In the dream, life had gone on and I was so happy to be Ella's mummy and so joyous in her arrival and her development, that it was as if all the sadness around Coran had gone to the point of being forgotten. I know that Coran will never be forgotten. I wear my 'angel pin' (the brooch made in Coran's memory) on my left side, close to my heart, every day – even if I'm just wearing an old T-shirt – and that helps me to feel close to Coran. Ella and Coran are the first thing I think about when I wake up in the morning and the last I think about before I go to sleep. When I wake up in the night, it's the same – they are both equally on my mind all the time. But more and more thoughts of my future with Ella are also coming into play now. They're wonderful thoughts and they help me to leave the sadness behind. I guess I'm just not quite sure if I want to yet.

It's strange to be nearly 36 weeks' pregnant! I really didn't think we'd get this far. It seemed that the risk of very premature delivery was so high after Coran's heart stopped beating that I'd resigned myself to having a premature baby and dealing with all that entailed. I'd got so used to that idea that now I feel almost overdue! I feel good physically though. My belly now measures 45 inches all the way around and I'm beginning to feel heavy. My legs ache and my fingers are swollen so that all my rings have had to come off! Most days I can't wear my watch past lunchtime due to the swelling! Turning over in bed is now a major operation and maintaining my balance whilst putting on my knickers is particularly challenging! But I'm enjoying it. I really like it. I'm so happy to feel that I'm growing. It was so strange in those weeks after Coran died; when I felt like I was getting smaller instead of bigger and even woke up some mornings with that really strong sensation that my belly was totally flat. In those weeks, it was as if my body was adjusting from being a twin pregnancy, and therefore 'big for dates', to a singleton pregnancy and it seems like it wasn't until a couple of weeks ago that things evened out.

Ella is clearly now using up all the space available to her. She doesn't really kick now but rather she nudges. Often I can see the outline of a foot or an elbow protruding or making its way along the contours of my belly. It's great to see and incredible to feel. I'll miss that when she's born. Mostly, she's a pretty calm babe though. And she nearly always stops moving as soon as somebody else places their hand on my tummy to feel her move! (She's very uncooperative in that regard!) She's been getting hic-ups loads too; at least once a day, and sometimes as much as four times a day! It took me ages to work out what the tiny rhythmic sensation was and then I read in a book that hic-ups are common at this gestational age. I can't imagine why unless it's somehow meant to strengthen the diaphragm in preparation for breathing. It's ever so cute!

I think my body is getting prepared for labour. I've had quite a lot of Braxton-Hicks contractions and had an hour or so last week where I really thought labour had started! I had a very strong B-H contraction, which I felt like a wave coming up over my belly. Then, when I was walking back from work, I started to get pain in my lower back too, to the point that I really had to waddle my way home! It was exciting though! A cup of tea and half an hour on the sofa made it stop, but I can't help but think that perhaps it was a little trial-run in preparation for the Big Day. I hope it's not too long now. And I really hope Ella decides to make an entrance before I get induced at 38 weeks.

I've been reading up on how one can encourage labour to start naturally. I've decided to continue working up until the end of next week and then take a week doing everything I can to encourage Ella to come into the world. I've read about everything from drinking castor oil (urgh) to having hot curries and lots of sex! Mum knows a good reflexologist too who may be able to encourage things to get started so I'll book an appointment with her for that 37th week. Anything is worth a try and it would have to be better than a hospital induction.

Although I'm now looking forward to the delivery and am feeling positive that I'll be able to cope with the physical realities of labour and birth and the emotional realities of delivering both our babies, a new anxiety has cropped up. I'm worried that the midwives who deliver the babies won't be as prepared as we are for what Coran may look like. I don't know why it worries me. I suppose I don't want to be aware that they are shocked or disturbed. I don't know why that matters to me but I know that it would make it harder for me if I got any sense of that. Julie, the community midwife visited last week and I voiced this concern to her. She said that she's hoping to be there at the birth if at all possible. That would be wonderful. She's been with us all the way on this journey, since our first booking-in appointment when I was 11 weeks' pregnant! So to end the journey with her there would be perfect. She can't promise that she'll be there, but I can hope! Mavis has also said that she'll be there if she can. If it was Jeremy, my Mum, Mavis and Julie at the delivery, it would be as perfect as it could be in terms of the love and support that I'd feel. That would make it so much easier to deal with the situation positively. It feels good to have hopes again and be able to envisage scenarios that would be preferable. Up until relatively recently, I really had no hopes; only expectations of difficulties and sadness.

Jeremy is continuing to be a fabulous husband. He's massaging my aching feet daily (wonderful!) and hardly grumbling at all when I ask him to run around the house getting things for me! He's happy that I feel better emotionally and he seems lighter now that he's relieved of the burden of being so strong for both of us. He's going to be a fantastic dad. He feels Coran's presence often, which is a great comfort to me. I hope that I will too, with time.

24th August – Here's hoping

It's now a week since we had our last appointment with the obstetrician and I still feel good! I had thought that perhaps my mood would plummet again after the appointment, as it has done in the past, but not this time! We have a plan of action now. If I don't go into spontaneous labour beforehand, I will be induced on Friday 2nd September. It is a relief. I had got very anxious on the way to the hospital, mostly in case the consultant changed his mind about letting me go past 38 weeks. I realised that I had attached so much hope and anticipation on knowing that the pregnancy would end at 38 weeks, that to be told that it may be *another two weeks* was an almost unbearable thought.

I feel guilty for that in some way. As a mother, I only want what is best for Ella. But what happens if that conflicts with what I want or need? Obviously, Ella takes priority now. That is a given. According to the experts, in this situation, what is best for me also happens to be best for Ella. Thankfully!

So only 9 days to go!

Having spent months anticipating and doing everything to prevent premature labour, I'm now doing all that I can to encourage spontaneous labour before next Friday! It's a funny old world; how things can swing from one extreme to the other. So I'm booked for acupuncture and reflexology; I'm doing nightly visualisations; I'm reciting over and over in my mind, "My cervix is shortening and dilating!"; I'm drinking raspberry leaf tea and taking blackcurrant oil tablets; and if it wasn't for a very painful hip that I've had since Saturday, I'd be going for lots of long walks! I'm drawing the line though at castor oil and orange juice. Urgh! Anything is worth a try… within reason!

Back to last Wednesday. The appointment with the consultant was overall very positive. He even said that if the induction goes well, he sees no reason why I shouldn't be able to labour and deliver in the birthing pool. That would be really fabulous. It's great to have hopes again about the delivery. For so many weeks, the delivery itself was just the inevitable hurdle that at some point had to be overcome one way or another. I couldn't even imagine anything 'good' or 'better' about the different options and possible outcomes. Now I am looking forward to the birth and I have hopes again! I hope that I'll go into spontaneous labour before next Friday. I hope that I'll be able to use the birthing pool. I hope that I'll be able to deliver the babies 'naturally'. Having totally accepted the 'fact' that I was going to have a caesarean section, I am now at peace with the possibility that the delivery may not go smoothly and that a section may be the safest thing for Ella and I. If that happens, then so be it. *Que sera, sera.*

There was a very sad aspect to last Wednesday that I have tried not to think about too much. But I have to write about it to stay truthful. Much to my disappointment and sadness, the ultrasonographer couldn't find Coran on the scan. (S)he was nowhere to be seen. Coran's little body won't have disappeared completely but the amniotic sac surrounding her will have been totally reabsorbed by my body by now and as Ella grows big and strong, she is squashing Coran out of the way. It was so very, very sad not to see Coran on the scan. I managed to hold myself together though and focus on how well Ella was doing (she was estimated to be 6 lbs) but it was so hard. It just seems impossible that this little person who is so very real to me cannot be seen on the scan monitor.

I have thought long and hard about why it is so important to me to see Coran. I haven't come to any definite answers but I think it's something to do with simply acknowledging her existence. I fear that others won't consider Coran 'important' or 'significant' if there is no body that marks her brief physical existence. It is as if her existence can be denied if there is no body to 'prove' it; as if it was all some terrible nightmare or delusion if there is no physical evidence. But I have the scan pictures to prove it! And I have been looking at them a lot this week. We saw Coran moving and kicking inside me and we heard two heart beats on several occasions. How can that just disappear into nothing? I am still struggling with this. I believe that the physical body is just the 'envelope' that the soul inhabits for a temporary time so I don't know why it seems so important to me. Perhaps it's just a reflection of the reality that Coran is still with me in physical form. Perhaps after the delivery I will find peace with this as I have with other aspects of Coran's existence and passing. As with so many things in this pregnancy, only time will tell.

So we have a maximum of nine days left to prepare for being parents. And our last day without our baby will be my birthday! Jeremy has taken time off from the 1st September, so we'll do something nice together on my birthday… something that we won't be able to do for a while once we have a babe in arms! We're not sure what that is yet, but we'll think of something! Of course, I may be in the hospital by then. How lovely it would be if Ella arrived on my birthday.

(She may not be so happy to share her birthday with mum for the rest of her life though!) I couldn't ask for a more wonderful birthday present than a healthy baby daughter. Here's hoping.

11th September – And she arrives!

It's been exactly one week and five hours since Ella Violet Blanche Smith was born! I can't believe how quickly the time has gone! Needless to say, she's absolutely gorgeous, fascinating, beautiful and perfect in every way. Getting her here was somewhat of an ordeal though! The induction process was generally not a success and despite taking the first dose of prostin (a synthetic prostaglandin pessary) on Friday morning, she didn't appear until 11:53am on Sunday 4th September, with the aid of both ventouse and forceps! It wasn't quite the peaceful, natural birth I had hoped for her, but she seems perfectly content and calm. She weighed 7 pounds, 2 ounces and had a full head of dark brown hair! What a beauty.

There were a few scary moments immediately after she was born; she was put onto my tummy but was floppy and had to be resuscitated. She was breathing within the minute though and I will never forget the sound of her first cry! What an incredible sound! There is no comparing it. Despite the two and a half days of labour, it all seemed so sudden when it came to it. One moment we were pregnant and the next moment our little darling daughter had been born and we had become a family!

After her birth, and when everybody was sure she was OK (about ten people had appeared in the room by this time), the ultrasound machine was brought into the delivery room to locate Coran. She couldn't be seen on the scan. However, she was born at 12:05 pm, along with the placenta, weighing just 80 grams. Jeremy took some photos of her which he showed me before I saw her in person. Although she didn't look like a 'normal' baby, she was quite obviously a baby – just very tiny, fragile and with darker skin. She had obviously been squashed somewhat by her growing sister but her arms, legs, fingers, toes and, with a bit of imagination, her face could all be clearly seen. And she is definitely a girl. I wasn't shocked, horrified or scared to see her. On the contrary; I was delighted to see her and hold her. Our tiny little baby girl.

Just after Coran was born, Ella was suckling her first Sunday lunch! What an incredible feeling! It felt so natural. I was exhausted after two sleepless, and painful nights, but when I looked into her big blue eyes, I found a part of myself that had never had the opportunity or necessity to surface before. I cannot say that she's 'mine'. It is true that Jeremy and I created her but she is not 'ours'. In fact, we are absolutely hers. We have been given the task of looking after her to the best of our ability and we are honoured and blessed. I hope we can live up to the task. When I look at her, I see a totally independent person who has come to this world and into our lives. I hope that we are able to give her everything that she needs and deserves and that we can give her the loving and happy home that is her birthright.

We spent the rest of the Sunday getting to know our baby daughter. The staff at the hospital were all fantastic and were happy to find us a private room so that we could keep Coran with us as well. I was hot, hungry, tired, sore, bruised and dizzy from the delivery and all the drugs that I'd been given, but to look at Ella filled me with such a feeling that my own wants and needs were immediately superseded by those of this little person. To sit up in bed and take her out of her crib was agonisingly painful but I was filled with such euphoria when I held her to my chest, looked into her eyes and stroked her cheek that the discomfort became completely insignificant.

Ella's head was misshapen due to the ventouse procedure and she had bruises on her face due to the forceps. By Monday, the bruising had nearly entirely gone and by Wednesday her head was perfectly shaped again. (I suspect that my taking lots and lots of *Arnica* had something to do with the fast recovery.) She got a bit of jaundice on Tuesday that has nearly entirely gone now thanks to regular feeding and lying her in natural light for a couple of hours each day. The last 24 hours, she has been feeding every two hours (I guess she's having a growth spurt!) and her umbilical cord fell off last night. I just can't believe she is a week old.

Ella is such a good baby! She rarely cries and when she does, she is easily appeased by a cuddle from mummy or daddy. Considering the traumatic pregnancy and birth that she experienced, she is surprisingly calm and content. Perhaps after the trauma she's already tolerated, she is pleasantly surprised by the peacefulness of the outside world!

It's difficult to describe the feeling of being a new parent. On the one hand, it feels a completely natural progression; this is the way it is meant to be and I sometimes feel like we're taking parenthood in our stride. But then I think back to last week and realise how completely different things are now. It's different but better, more wonderful, more fascinating and absolutely the only way it could be!

I have had a few moments when I wonder what it would be like if I had both my little girls in my arms. I am particularly reminded of this when Ella feeds with her body tucked under my arm – in the classic twin feeding position, which oddly she seems to favour. I guess I will always have moments like that. I wonder too whether they are identical or fraternal twins and, if they are identical, what it would have been like to have two babies as beautiful as Ella. The hospital consultant is currently looking into the possibility of genetic testing to determine their zygosity. Geneticists at St George's Hospital in Tooting have been contacted and are investigating the situation. Surprisingly, they have never had a request like this before. If Ella is anything like me when she is older, then she will want answers to questions and will want to know whether she and her sister were identical. So I feel I owe it to her to try to find out. In the meantime, of course, Coran's cremation is being delayed but hopefully we'll have an answer regarding the post-mortem in the next day or two and will be able to lay Coran's body to rest shortly.

It will be strange to close this chapter. It feels like I was pregnant for a lifetime! I know though that the next chapter will be a joyous one and I will savour every moment. I have been forever changed by our experience and 'normal' will never be the same again. But I am richer for it. I will always be reminded of Coran whenever I see rose quartz, heart symbols, acorns, roses and especially white butterflies or a crescent moon looking down at us. I will be reminded of what could have been whenever I see or hear about twins. And yet to have Ella in my life is to be the richest woman alive. I wouldn't change anything. I would do it all again. I would go through the whole process and more if it meant I would have Ella with me in my life. She is my world.

Postscript

A cremation was conducted on 26th September, three weeks after Ella and Coran were born. I wrote a letter to Coran, which my sister bravely read out. My father read a beautiful eulogy (see below). Eva Cassidy's rendition of "Somewhere Over the Rainbow" played whilst Coran's pretty white coffin moved through the curtain. We shared the ceremony with family and closest friends. Ella, of course, was there too.

At the time of writing, Coran's ashes are kept in a tiny box within a burgundy velvet bag. I hope that one day Ella and her identical twin brothers, Kayden and Brynley (born 2nd February 2007) will join me in scattering their sister's ashes.

Ella has known about Coran since Day 1. We chose to ensure that there was never a big day that we revealed the story to her. Every year, on 19th June, "Coran's Day", the children and I release balloons up to heaven. They have recently taken to attaching little notes to the balloon string. We have a special ornament to hang on the Christmas tree, which reminds us of Coran. Ella has a glass angel statue that my mother gave her on her first Christmas, which she holds when she misses her sister. She has two intertwined candles that she sometimes chooses to light when thinking of her sister.

At age 4, Ella went through a grieving crisis. Although I considered the possibility that I was projecting my own grief, I am positive that Ella was going through very real feelings of loss and grief. It lasted about 6 weeks, during which she would draw and paint images of angels in the sky; she would cry on me for up to an hour, that big, shoulder-shaking grief cry; she would ask questions about why her sister died; she would fantasise about how it would have been if she'd survived.

To date, Coran is very much a part of the family, who happens to not be here with us on Earth. She will never be forgotten.

Sadly, our marriage broke up. The further strain of another high-risk pregnancy (Ella was just 9 months when we conceived twins) and the very real stresses of raising three children under 18 months, were ultimately too much for our relationship to survive. We remain friends, intent on offering our children the best we can.

Thank you, dear reader, for allowing me to share my story. If you or a loved one are going through a similar process, please do feel free to get in touch. You can email me at vicky@thelovingparent.com or find me on Twitter @TheLovingParent.

If you are grieving, I wish you the strength to carry you through the process and hope that you will find peace when you are ready.

To my darling daughter, Coran

This is the hardest letter I have ever had to write. There are so many things I want to say to you and yet I am at a loss for words.

You lived for a grand 27 weeks inside me. Thank you so much for choosing me. My life is so much richer for having known you, even for that short time. I will always remember you kicking me on the right side of my tummy, just under my ribs. I will always remember you and your sister kicking me in response to me talking to you both. I will remember walking in the woods when the Spring birds were singing – hoping beyond hope that you might be able to hear their beautiful song but all along aware that perhaps your brain hadn't developed sufficiently for you to be able to recognise the sounds. It broke my heart to think about how limited your experience of life was, and it still does.

But despite the limits placed on you, in your unique and extremely special way, you have taught me so much. The lessons I have learned from you have changed me forever and will always be with me. You will always be with me – in heart, mind, spirit, memory and soul.

Knowing that you were going to die was without doubt the hardest thing I have ever had to come to terms with. It is all so very unfair. I wonder why you chose a body that was never going to give you what I feel you deserved; a long, happy, healthy life with Ella, your Daddy and I. Now I know that you don't need to be here with us in body in order to live with us always. How I would love to hold you, cuddle you and comfort you but I will never have the chance.

I hope you know how much I love you. From the moment I saw the outline of two heads on that ultrasound scan, I have loved you. Did I sense your presence even before that scan? I think so. Somehow I knew that I was carrying twins. I just didn't know how to integrate that with the feeling that I'd only have one living child to care for later on. I hope you know how many people your little life has touched. But, above all, I hope that you got what you needed out of your life this time round and I hope that you could feel the love that your daddy and I have for you.

We will be cremating your little body a week tomorrow. It will be a final goodbye to your physical presence on this earth and yet it is the beginning of the rest of our lives together.

Watch over us from wherever you may be. Watch over your sister, Ella, and know that with each breath she takes and each milestone she reaches, I will think of you and wonder how it could have been. I wish you love, friendship and happiness and look forward to meeting you again when the time is right.

I love you.

Mummy

xx

To Coran, from your Grandfather

Vicky and Jeremy, thank you for asking me to say these words.

Your beautifully expressed letter to Coran, together with the pages of thoughts you have shared with us during these last weeks and months, have helped us understand your feelings. But, in the end, it was your journey, and the four of you travelled it together.

We have accompanied you as best we could, never quite knowing what to say or what to do. Now that journey ends, a new much longer one begins. Ella, we are so pleased and proud to have you with us today, so beautiful, so strong, so perfect.

But, this is not your day – for your whole life lies ahead. It is your sister's.

Coran, although you never really gave us the chance to say hello, we do have this unique opportunity to say goodbye.

But before we do, there is something we want to tell you - that your short time on earth was not wasted, nor will it be forgotten.

That your life had a reason we do not doubt, even though, for now, we may not know what that reason is. But we will.

Until then, we will think of you as an angel sent to watch over Ella. Thank you for helping her into this world.

She will always be grateful and so shall we.

Your life has touched us all. Those of us who were privileged to see you are glad that we did. You were beautiful, too, and you were born.

Therefore, in saying goodbye, we know you will not be far away and that you will live in our hearts forever.

Goodbye Coran, and thank you.

Pip
26th September, 2005

Loving
Parent

TheLovingParent.com
facebook.com/thelovingparent
twitter.com/thelovingparent

Printed in Great Britain
by Amazon